A Kid's Guide to

Keystone
Species
in Nature

Keystone Species that Live in the Sea & Along the Coastline

Bonnie Hinman

Mitchell Lane
PUBLISHERS

P.O. Box 196
Hockessin, DE 19707
www.mitchelllane.com

Mitchell Lane

PUBLISHERS

Printing   1   2   3   4   5   6   7   8

Keystone Species that Live in Deserts
Keystone Species that Live in Forests
Keystone Species that Live in Grasslands
Keystone Species that Live in the Mountains
Keystone Species that Live in Ponds, Streams, and Wetlands
Keystone Species that Live in the Sea and Along the Coastline

Library of Congress Cataloging-in-Publication Data
Hinman, Bonnie.
 Keystone species that live in the sea and along the coastline / by Bonnie Hinman.
    pages cm. — (A kid's guide to keystone species in nature)
 Includes bibliographical references and index.
 Audience: Ages 8-11.
 Audience: Grades 3-6.
 ISBN 978-1-68020-064-5 (library bound)
 1. Keystone species—Juvenile literature. 2. Marine ecology—Juvenile literature.
 I. Title.
 QH541.15.K48H563 2015
 577.2'6—dc23
                                                         2015008200

eBook ISBN: 978-1-68020-065-2

PBP

Contents

Words in **bold** throughout can be found in the Glossary.

Introduction

Most arches built today contain a single building block at the top that is the most important piece. This special piece can be found in the arches of soaring cathedrals, doorways in temples, and even simple buildings made out of wooden blocks. It is called a keystone, and it holds everything else together. Remove the keystone and the building or doorway is likely to collapse.

The same thing is true in nature. Certain species of animals and plants are so important to their **ecosystems**, that if they disappear, the whole system may collapse. They are called keystone species.

Some keystone species are large, like tiger sharks, while others are small, like Antarctic krill. But size doesn't matter in an ecosystem. All living things rely on

A keystone of a palace archway

Sea otter

other species to survive. A keystone species plays an especially large role that affects many different species in an ecosystem. Some keystone species are at the top of a huge ecosystem like the Greater Yellowstone Ecosystem, while others may affect a tiny ecosystem in a river or forest. Whether the ecosystem is big or small, the result of a keystone species disappearing or being greatly reduced is the same. Just like one falling domino can cause many others to fall, the loss of a keystone species can lead to the extinction of many other species.

Today scientists are focusing more attention on preserving the natural balance in ecosystems. Identifying and protecting keystone species is an important part of their work.

Chapter 1
TIGER SHARK

Tiger sharks are scary fish. They will eat anything, including people. But tiger sharks do not begin their day by deciding to hunt for a tasty person to chomp on. They probably would prefer to find a **dugong** to eat for breakfast. However, if a person shows up in a hungry tiger shark's path, it might decide to take a bite.

The news seems to travel fast when a tiger shark kills a person, but events like these are actually rare. In Hawaii, for example, fewer than ten people are attacked by sharks in an average year. Most of these victims are injured but not killed.[1] Meanwhile, an average of fifty-two people drown each year in Hawaiian oceans.[2]

Tiger sharks live all over the world in tropical and subtropical waters. They often live in coastal waters, but scientists have learned that they may also spend many months in the open ocean.[3]

Adult tiger sharks average between 10 and 14 feet (3.25 and 4.25 meters) long, but they can be as long as 25 feet (7.5 meters). The weight of an adult tiger shark ranges from 850 pounds (385 kilograms) to 2,000 pounds (900 kilograms) or more.

A tiger shark cruises the bottom of the ocean near Hawaii. Scientists used to think that tiger sharks patrolled only shallow coastal waters. Research using small transmitters attached to tiger sharks told a different story. Tracking showed that tiger sharks sometimes swam long distances to spend part of their lives in the open ocean.

Young tiger sharks have tiger-like stripes and spots, which fade as they grow. Adults are grey or blue-green with a white or yellowish-white belly. Their heads are wedge shaped and their noses are **blunt**. They have **serrated** teeth that they use to tear into their prey's flesh. Powered by strong jaws, these teeth can also crack the bones and shells of their prey.

Tiger sharks can live as long as fifty years in the wild, but their average lifespan is twenty-seven years. Although many animals live longer in captivity than they do in the wild, tiger sharks actually have a much shorter lifespan in captivity. The longest a tiger shark can be expected to live in captivity is seventeen to twenty years. Scientists aren't sure why this is true, but they know that in the wild a tiger shark may swim many miles in a day. Even the largest tanks do not give them the space to do this. Instead of catching their food naturally, captive sharks are fed dead food. Scientists think they prefer live food, so they won't eat as much in captivity and may eventually die of starvation.[4]

Where Tiger Sharks Are Found

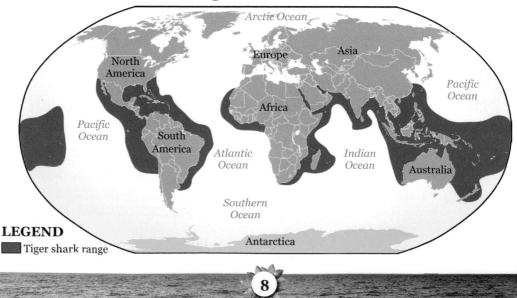

LEGEND
Tiger shark range

Tiger Shark Pups

Male and female tiger sharks do not form pairs except to mate. Tiger sharks spend most of their time alone, although sometimes they will share a large prey for dinner. Both males and females are ready to breed once they reach a certain size. For females, that size is about 8.2 to 11.5 feet (2.5 to 3.5 meters) long. Males are mature at about 7.4 to 9.5 feet long (2.3 to 2.9 meters).[5]

Tiger sharks give birth in an unusual way. The babies, called pups, develop in eggs inside the mother. The eggs hatch while still in the mother's body, and the pups are born soon afterward. The mother shark may have ten to eighty-two pups per **litter**. The pups are twenty to thirty-five inches (fifty-one to ninety centimeters) long when they are born.[6]

The **gestation** period for tiger sharks is very long—thirteen to sixteen months. Females usually have litters only once every three years. Pups are on their own immediately after birth. They grow slowly, so in their early years they are easy prey for other sharks and for humans. Tiger sharks are born in nursery areas, which give them some protection. The pups' camouflage tiger stripes and natural speed also help them escape predators.[7]

What's for Dinner

Tiger sharks will eat almost anything including plastic bottles, pieces of boats, clothing, tires, and any other kind of garbage that comes their way. But the foods they like best include sea turtles, bony fish, sea birds, squid, and dugongs. Their ability to eat almost anything is what helps tiger sharks maintain their size. They need a lot of food because they are so big. Unfortunately, their big appetite also means that tiger sharks can be dangerous to humans. People should stay out of the water if a tiger shark is spotted nearby.

Tiger sharks have organs called ampullae (am-PUHL-uh) of Lorenzini to help them find prey. Filled with a jelly-like substance, the organs are located on the ends of their noses, and can detect electromagnetic fields. When fish and other animals move, their muscles give off electrical signals. The sharks' ability to sense these signals gives them an advantage in hunting prey. Tiger sharks

This huge dugong is a vegetarian. It eats underwater grasses in oceans day and night to maintain its size. A dugong is a mammal and breathes air. It can stay underwater as long as six minutes before coming up for air. The dugong is related to the manatee and the elephant.

may also use these organs to sense Earth's magnetic fields and find their way through the ocean. Tiger sharks have lateral lines running along the sides of their bodies. These lines are sensitive to vibrations in the water from nearby animals. Both of these senses let the sharks know where other sharks are. When several tiger sharks are feeding on a single carcass, they can send out signals to let the others know who is in charge—and who will eat first.[8]

Apex Predators
Tiger sharks are **apex predators**, which means they have no enemies except man. Since they eat so much, they have a large effect on their ecosystem. Tiger sharks keep their prey from overwhelming the **habitat**. Too many animals of any kind can upset the balance in an ecosystem.

Scientists have discovered that not only do apex predators like tiger sharks eat prey; they also scare some animals away from an area. Bottlenose dolphins stay away from places with lots of tiger sharks, even though tiger sharks don't eat bottlenose dolphins very often.

In Shark Bay, Australia, scientists studied dugongs and tiger sharks. They found that dugongs eat in different areas when tiger sharks are present. When few tiger sharks are around, dugongs prefer to graze in the middle of seagrass meadows, where there is plenty of good grass. But the meadows' edges are close to deep water, where a dugong can dive quickly to escape a tiger shark. Even though the grass is not as good there, a dugong will eat at the edges of meadows more often when tiger sharks are around. Since tiger sharks don't live in the same place all year, each part of the meadow gets a chance to grow back when the dugongs aren't eating there. That keeps the meadows healthy, which is important to the **benthic** animals that live in them.[9]

For many of the animals that live at the bottom of the ocean, seagrass meadows provide protection from predators and strong ocean currents. Some of these animals, like clams, mussels, and oysters, actually remove pollution and bacteria from the ocean water as they eat. Without tiger sharks, our oceans could become unhealthy very quickly.

Tiger sharks are officially listed as near threatened. There are plenty of them right now, but if people around the world continue catching them in the numbers that they do today, the species could become endangered soon. Some fishers catch tiger sharks when they are fishing for other fish. Other fishers try to catch tiger sharks to sell for several products. The fins, skin, and liver oil are the most valuable parts of a tiger shark.

Shark fin soup is a great **delicacy** in China. Because of this, the fins bring a high price on their own. Fishermen don't want to carry the entire shark on their boats, so they cut off the fin and throw the rest of the shark back into the water. **Conservationists** especially want to stop this practice, called finning. Killing tiger sharks just for their fins is illegal along many coastlines.

Tiger sharks are not animals that anyone wants to come face-to-face with, but they play an important role as a keystone species in their environments. If they continue to decline in number, our oceans could be in a lot of trouble. But by controlling the way that tiger sharks are fished, we can ensure that they are around to patrol our coastlines for many years to come.

Megalodon: The Megatooth Shark

The megalodon lived until around two million years ago in the Pleistocene (PLAHY-stuh-seen) **Epoch**. It likely became extinct long before woolly mammoths roamed the earth. Based on fossil records, scientists think that some megalodons may have been as long as sixty-six feet (twenty meters).[10] Whale sharks, which are the biggest sharks today, seldom grow to forty feet (twelve meters) long. Stories persist that these extinct megatooth sharks still roam the deep waters of our oceans. During Shark Week 2013, Discovery Channel aired a show about finding the megalodon. Angry scientists and fans said the show was misleading because it said that megalodons might still exist. Discovery ended the show with a note that said that some events and people were **dramatized**.

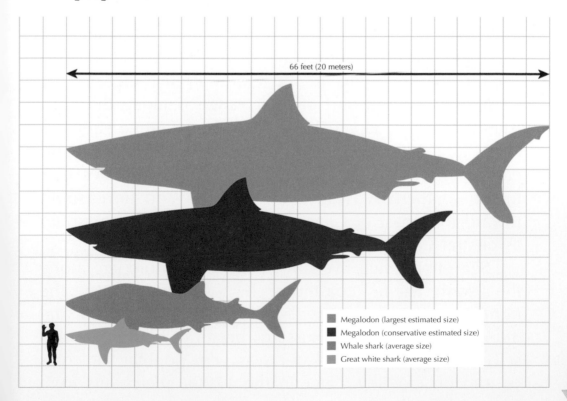

66 feet (20 meters)

■ Megalodon (largest estimated size)
■ Megalodon (conservative estimated size)
■ Whale shark (average size)
■ Great white shark (average size)

Chapter 2

SEA OTTER

If you had hair as thick as a sea otter, you would need a very strong comb to style your hair. Your scalp has about 1,300 hairs in 1 square inch, or 6.45 square centimeters (but some people have slightly more or less).[1] But a sea otter can have more than 900,000 hairs on just one square inch of its body.[2] That's the thickest hair of any mammal.

There are three subspecies of sea otters and they all live in coastal waters in the North Pacific Ocean. The most southwestern part of their **range** is along the Kuril Islands north of Japan. From there, their range stretches north to the Commander Islands off Russia's coast and east to the Aleutian Islands. Their range continues east to the southern Alaskan coastal waters and turns south toward the coast of Canada. The otters live as far south as central California.

Sea otters once lived in much larger numbers along the North Pacific coastlines. In the early 1700s, the number of otters worldwide was between 150,000 and 300,000.[3] In the 1700s Russians began to hunt otters and sell their **pelts**. The thick fur was very popular for coats or trim on clothing. Later in the 1700s, merchants from many other countries started hunting sea otters or buying

This female sea otter and her nearly full-grown daughter spend most of their time swimming in the ocean. Sea otters may come on shore during storms or if there are too many other otters swimming in the ocean.

their pelts from Native Americans. They did not stop hunting until there were no more otters to find. Sea otters were almost extinct by the beginning of the twentieth century. In 1911, the United States, Great Britain, Russia, and Japan signed the International Fur Seal Treaty, which banned the hunting of sea otters.

The fur on sea otters was popular for good reasons. It is a beautiful brown or reddish brown and very warm. Sea otters have two layers of fur: a dark, thick undercoat and lighter-colored, longer guard hairs. The waterproof guard hairs keep water from reaching the undercoat, and the undercoat traps a layer of air next to the otter's skin. This air keeps the otter warm. Sea otters do not have extra fat to keep their bodies warm like many other marine mammals do. Since they live in cold water, they could not survive without their fur.

Sea otters are in the same family of animals as skunks, ferrets, and weasels. But they are larger than their land-

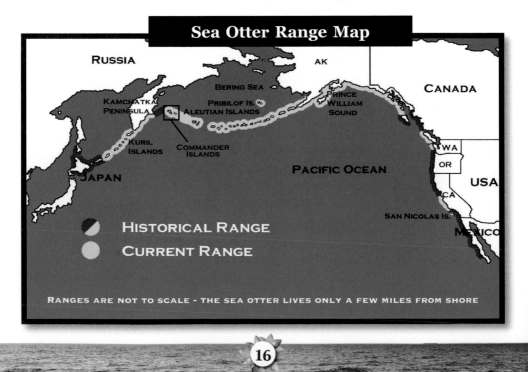

Sea Otter Range Map

RUSSIA

AK

BERING SEA

CANADA

KAMCHATKA PENINSULA
PRIBILOF IS.
ALEUTIAN ISLANDS
PRINCE WILLIAM SOUND

KURIL ISLANDS
COMMANDER ISLANDS

PACIFIC OCEAN

WA

OR

JAPAN

USA

CA

SAN NICOLAS IS.

MEXICO

HISTORICAL RANGE

CURRENT RANGE

RANGES ARE NOT TO SCALE - THE SEA OTTER LIVES ONLY A FEW MILES FROM SHORE loving cousins. Adult sea otters can weigh from thirty-one to ninety-nine pounds (fourteen to forty-five kilograms). They are usually 3 to 5 feet (1 to 1.5 meters) long. Female otters are smaller than males.

That's a Lot of Food!

Sea otters like to eat. And it's a good thing, since they need to eat at least 25 percent of their body weight every day.[4] For a sixty-pound sea otter, that's at least fifteen pounds of food in a day. That's how much food it takes to keep their bodies running in the cold waters where they live.

Sea otters are **carnivorous**. They eat sea urchins, clams, snails, abalone, crabs, mussels, octopus, fish, and many other species. But not all sea otters eat all of these foods. Sea otters have different favorite foods depending on what's available in their area. Some sea otters may prefer to dive in deep water for their food, and others may stay in shallow water. So one group of sea otters may eat lots of crabs and sea urchins while another group may eat mainly clams.

Sea otters hold their breath as they dive down to the bottom of the ocean to look for food, usually in a group. They have sensitive whiskers that can detect small animals that are hidden from view. They catch their prey with their paws and tuck them into some loose folds of skin under their armpits. These folds are like shopping bags for the sea otters.

Once back on the surface of the ocean, the otters flip onto their backs and use their stomachs like floating tables. An otter will use a stone as a tool if it needs to open the shell of a clam or crab. The otter hits the shell to break it open, and the meat inside takes a short trip to the otter's mouth.

Sea Otter Family Life

Baby sea otters, or pups, are born year-round. Females usually give birth once a year although it can be every other year. They typically have only one pup at a time. Most females begin to breed at around four years old, while males become mature at five or six years old. A female sea otter shows no signs of pregnancy until the day before delivery, when she may eat less than usual. Birth is a simple process. The female rolls in the water and comes up with a pup in her teeth.[5]

A sea otter pup spends much of the next two months on its mother's chest. It nurses and sleeps there while Mom floats in the water. If the pup should fall off, it

This female sea otter looks curious to see who is looking at her. Her small pup is comfortable resting on her chest. Sea otters rarely have twins because the mother can only care for one baby at a time. The second pup will not survive.

cannot sink because it has so much air in its fur. The pup's mother may wrap it in kelp (a type of algae) to keep it in one place while she dives underwater to look for food. Pups begin diving themselves when they are about two months old. They remain with their mother for about six to eight months.

Sea otters are social animals that live in groups called rafts or pods. Males stay together in their own groups, while females and their pups form separate groups. Male sea otters do not help take care of their pups. Males and females usually only come together to breed.

A Keystone Species in Danger

Sea otters have several natural predators including great white sharks, bald eagles, and coyotes. Killer whales have also been seen eating sea otters, but scientists suspect that sea otters are not part of the killer whales' natural diet. It is possible that humans have hunted too many of the killer whales' favorite foods, forcing them to start eating sea otters instead.[6]

Off the coast of California, sea otters have been getting sick and even dying from **parasites** that normally only infect cats and opossums. Scientists don't know how these parasites are getting into the ocean, but they think that people could be responsible. It is possible that parasites made it to the ocean after people flushed infected cat litter down the toilet. The way people have changed and built on the land near the ocean could be causing the parasites to wash into the ocean along with rainwater.[7]

Even though sea otters have been internationally protected for over a hundred years, they are still endangered. Sea otters are very sensitive to disease and pollution in their environment. Oil spills are especially dangerous for sea otters. The oil causes their fur to mat, eliminating the layer of air that protects them against the cold ocean water. When the oil-soaked sea otters try to groom themselves, they can also end up eating the oil in their fur in the process.[8]

Sea otters play a big role in keeping kelp forests healthy. Kelp is a large, brown seaweed that grows in groups in the ocean's shallow waters. A kelp plant grows from the rocky bottom of the ocean upward toward the surface. Kelp forests provide food and protection to many species of fish, **invertebrates**, mammals, and birds. Sea urchins especially like to eat kelp and can destroy a kelp forest if their population grows too large. Sea otters love to eat sea urchins, so there are fewer sea urchins and more healthy kelp forests anywhere sea otters live.

Although sea otters are slowly recovering in the North Pacific, they are not safe from extinction just yet. To protect the sea otters, the kelp forests, and all the animals that depend on them, we will need to make changes to keep our oceans cleaner. By keeping sea otters healthy, we can save an entire ecosystem.

Giant kelp grows in a thick forest off the Channel Islands of California.

Homer, the Famous Sea Otter

Homer was a young sea otter when she was rescued after an oil spill in Alaska in 1989. The oil tanker *Exxon Valdez* had run into an underwater **reef** in Prince William Sound. At least ten million gallons of oil spilled into the water. The oil killed as many as 5,500 sea otters in the months that followed the spill. Oil from the spill is still in the ocean today. Found near Homer, Alaska, the sea otter was oil-soaked and had swallowed oil as well. Rescuers saved Homer and about thirty-five other sea otters. Homer went to live at the Point Defiance Zoo and Aquarium in Tacoma, Washington. She was twenty-five years old when she died in 2013. Homer was the last known surviving otter of the oil spill disaster.[9]

US Navy Mechanized Landing Craft (LCM) are anchored along the shoreline as Navy and civilian personnel position hoses during oil clean-up efforts on Smith Island. The massive oil spill occurred when the commercial tanker Exxon Valdez *ran aground while transiting the waters of Prince William Sound on March 24, 1989.*

Chapter 3
ANTARCTIC KRILL

The dinner menu for blue whales is made up almost entirely of Antarctic krill. It is hard to imagine that a blue whale, which is the largest animal on earth, could make a meal from two-inch- (five-centimeter-) long invertebrates. As it turns out, it is not the size of the krill that makes a difference; it is the number of them. A blue whale lunges into a swarm of krill with his mouth open, takes in ocean water along with krill, and pushes the water out. Thousands of krill remain in his mouth. He promptly swallows them.

Antarctic krill are one of about eighty-five species of krill in the world. Scientists estimate that these **crustaceans** have the largest population of any species on Earth.[1] Antarctic krill live in the oceans surrounding Antarctica. This huge continent at the South Pole is a cold, icy place. There are no humans living there permanently, but some people do live there temporarily for scientific research. Antarctic krill can live in waters up to 2,000 feet (600 meters) deep. On average they live at about 500 feet (150 meters) deep.[2]

Antarctic krill are pinkish-red and transparent. They have large black eyes and their digestive system is visible

This antarctic krill has special organs that shine blue-green light, making the krill glow. When its lights are turned off, its pinkish color will be visible again. Scientists are not sure what krill use their light for, but they think that it may attract other krill for spawning, or help them to navigate through the water. This krill's latest green meal can be seen through its transparent exoskeleton near its eye.

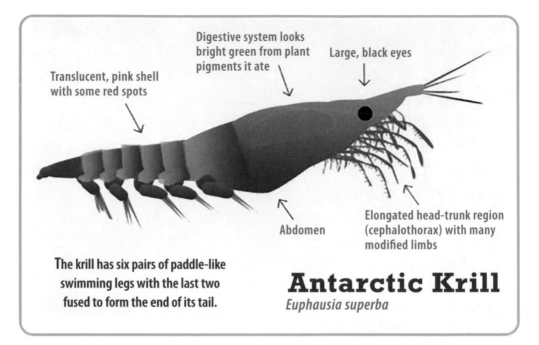

Digestive system looks bright green from plant pigments it ate

Large, black eyes

Translucent, pink shell with some red spots

Abdomen

Elongated head-trunk region (cephalothorax) with many modified limbs

The krill has six pairs of paddle-like swimming legs with the last two fused to form the end of its tail.

Antarctic Krill
Euphausia superba

through their shell. This hard shell is called an exoskeleton and has two parts: the cephalothorax (sef-uh-loh-THAWR-aks) and abdomen. A krill has six pairs of legs, but the last two legs are fused into a tail. It has two antennae, and ten light-producing organs called photophores (FOH-tuh-fohrz). Antarctic krill are between 2 and 2.6 inches (5 to 6.5 centimeters) long and weigh about 0.1 ounces (2 grams).[3]

An Antarctic krill usually eats phytoplankton (fahy-tuh-PLANGK-tuhn). These plants are so small that a person would need a microscope to see them. Phytoplankton live near the surface of the ocean where they can get enough sunlight to grow. At night, Antarctic krill swim upward toward the phytoplankton to feed. With small leg-like limbs that are attached to their cephalothoraxes, the krill form baskets to catch the phytoplankton. The basket is filled with water containing phytoplankton. After the water gets filtered out, the trapped phytoplankton are passed to the krill's mouth.

Development of an Antarctic Krill

Antarctic krill have an unusual life cycle that is adapted to the cold, dark waters of the southern oceans. After mating, female krill lay eggs several times between December and March, which is summer in the southern **hemisphere**. Females may lay as many as ten thousand eggs at one time.[4]

Once laid, the eggs sink slowly into the cold ocean for about ten days. They may float down as deep as 6,600 feet (2,000 meters) before hatching. When the eggs hatch into **larvae**, they begin a slow journey to the ocean surface. As they rise, the larvae molt for the first time. All crustaceans molt when they outgrow their shells. The old shell is shed, revealing a new one underneath.

The larvae go through several stages of development before they become juveniles. In early larval stages the krill eat their remaining yolk to survive. Once they reach surface waters, they eat phytoplankton. When winter arrives in Antarctica, much of the ocean is covered in ice. Antarctic krill survive their first winter by eating algae on the underside of the ice. Krill do not become adults until they are about two years old. They live five to seven years, on average. Adult krill have an unusual ability to shrink and become juvenile krill again. Scientists believe this is a way for the krill to survive the long, dark winter. They can use their own body **proteins** for food as they shrink. They molt in reverse, becoming smaller and losing all adult sexual characteristics. In spring the krill once again molt into adults and breed.

Swarms of Krill

Antarctic krill swim in large groups called schools or swarms. As many as thirty thousand krill may be found in 35 cubic feet (1 cubic meter) of water at any given moment. The most dense swarms can be seen from space. Scientists have discovered that some krill swarms may contain only juvenile krill. Other swarms may be all female or all male.[5]

Swarms or schools of krill have an average length of 330 feet (100 meters) but can be as long as 60 miles (100 kilometers).[6] That means that the average krill swarm is almost as long as a football field. A 60-mile-long swarm is longer than nine hundred football fields.

Although the large swarms make Antarctic krill appealing to large predators, swarming also protects the krill from smaller predators. A small animal that tries to eat one krill on its own would quickly get distracted by seeing so many krill moving at once. Krill have other ways of avoiding predators, too. If a predator appears, the krill in a swarm may all molt at the same time. The empty shells that suddenly fill the water can confuse the predators while the krill quickly swim away. Krill may also remain far below the ocean's surface in deep, cold water where their predators will not go.[7]

Fueling Antarctica's Oceans

Although they have defenses against some predators, Antarctic krill can't avoid every predator. Krill are the primary food for many whales, penguins, seals, and fish. If Antarctic krill were not around, many of their predators might not survive either. These predators might also start

This blue whale is a baleen whale. Baleen whales have plates hanging from their upper jaw that look like the teeth of a comb. The plates are strong and flexible like fingernails. Baleen whales use these plates to strain ocean water for food. Some other baleen whales are gray and humpback whales.

eating large numbers of other prey, which could disrupt the southern oceans' food chain.

Humans catch Antarctic krill to use as food on fish farms. They also use the krill to make medicines and health supplements. As demand for these products increases, some people worry that overfishing could endanger the krill. In 1982, an international commission was created to make sure that this doesn't happen. Fishing may not be the greatest threat to the tiny Antarctic krill, however.

Despite strict controls on fishing, the population of Antarctic krill may be up to 80 percent smaller than it was just thirty years ago.[8] Scientists think that climate change is reducing the sea ice that forms over the southern oceans each winter. Young Antarctic krill depend on the algae that live on the underside of this ice to make it through the winter. As the ice grows smaller and smaller, krill populations do the same.

Slow climate change is a natural process on Earth, but today the climate is changing rapidly. Some scientists believe that this is largely due to human activities, such as air pollution and destruction of natural resources like trees. Although some parts of Antarctica have actually gotten colder, temperatures along the west coast of the Antarctic Peninsula have been increasing rapidly over the last sixty years. This has affected the sea ice as well as the Antarctic krill populations there.

Antarctic krill may be tiny, but in many ways they are the fuel that runs the Antarctic waters. Without them, an entire ecosystem could change forever. However if humans can learn to care for and protect our Earth, we might be able to protect the Antarctic krill and their oceans, too.

This colony of Adélie penguins lives on Cape Royds, which is on the western edge of Ross Island, Antarctica. They build their nests in small depressions in the ground and line the nests with small stones to help keep their eggs dry. Adélie penguins are just one of many species whose favorite food is krill.

A Few Cold Facts
About Antarctica

1. Antarctica is the coldest place on Earth. The average annual temperatures there are around 14 degrees Fahrenheit (-10 degrees Celsius) on the coast and -76 degrees Fahrenheit (-60 degrees Celsius) inland. The lowest recorded temperature on Earth is -136 degrees Fahrenheit (-93 degrees Celsius), measured by NASA on the East Antarctic Plateau on August 10, 2010.

2. Days and nights can be very different in Antarctica than they are at most other places on Earth. At the South Pole, the sun can be seen all day from September to March, and sets from May until July. Heading north from the South Pole, days and nights become slightly more normal. However much of Antarctica experiences at least a few weeks when the sun never sets or never fully rises.

3. Scientists study ice cores in Antarctica. The ice there has been built up over many years, so the deepest ice is also the oldest. By drilling down into the layers of ice, scientists learn about the changes in Earth's temperatures and gases in the atmosphere over time. The oldest core ever drilled contained ice that was about eight hundred thousand years old.

Two scientists drill ice cores in the Antarctic ice.

Chapter 4
RED MANGROVE

Have you ever seen a tree walk? The red mangrove tree doesn't actually go anywhere, but it is sometimes called a walking tree. A red mangrove has lots of prop roots that emerge from the tree trunk above the ground, and grow down into the soil. These roots make the mangrove look like it is about to walk along the coastline where it lives.

There are about seventy mangrove species in the world.[1] Mangrove trees are evergreen and can live in muddy, waterlogged soil. They grow in salt water and in brackish water, which is a combination of salt and fresh water. Mangroves can survive even when their roots are completely underwater.

Red mangroves cannot **tolerate** freezing temperatures, so they live in places with tropical and subtropical climates. This includes many islands in the Caribbean Sea. Red mangroves are common on the coasts of Florida. They also grow on the western coast of Africa and the east and west coasts of several South and Central American countries. Red mangroves can grow to 115 feet (35 meters) or more in the warmest areas. At the far northern and far southern edges of their range, the trees average 20 feet (6 meters) because of the cooler temperatures.

This red mangrove is growing in a shallow section of the Caribbean Sea near the coast of Panama. Most trees absorb oxygen from the soil surrounding their roots, but the wet soil under the water doesn't contain much oxygen. A red mangrove's prop roots grow above the soil and water so they can absorb oxygen from the air. This allows the tree to grow underwater, where other trees cannot.

Walking Roots

A red mangrove doesn't just grow taller; it also grows wider. As more prop roots are added, the base of the tree expands outward. This is why red mangroves look like they are walking.

Prop roots anchor the tree firmly in place. The roots also trap silt and debris, creating new layers of soil. Most red mangroves live in areas where the tides come in from the ocean and then go back out a few hours later. The constant movement of tidal waters builds up the soil around the trees' roots.

The red mangroves' **aerial** prop roots help the trees take in oxygen. Most plant roots get oxygen from the soil around them. But underground red mangrove roots live in airless, waterlogged soil. So the mangroves' aerial prop roots must collect oxygen from the air and send it down to the underground roots.

Flowers and Propagules

Red mangrove flowers have both male and female parts. This allows them to self-pollinate in order to reproduce. A red mangrove produces its first flowers when it is about five years old. The flowers have four yellowish sepals and four white and brown cotton-like petals. The trees bloom all year long, but more flowers appear during the wet season or spring and summer seasons.[2]

The brown fruit that grows from the flower is about 1 to 2 inches (2.5 to 5 centimeters) long. Although most plants release their seeds before germination, the red mangrove fruit begins to germinate while it is still on the parent plant. This process is called vivipary (vahy-VIP-uh-ree). A propagule (PROP-uh-gyool) emerges from the fruit and continues to grow for three to six months. By the time the propagule is ready to leave the parent tree, it is about eight to fourteen inches (twenty to thirty-five centimeters) long. The propagule can be green, reddish, or brownish, but the lower part is always brown.

Red mangrove propagules eventually fall off the trees and float in the water. At first the propagules float on their sides. As the brown tips absorb water, roots begin to sprout after ten to thirty days. The propagules then turn to an upright position. This change makes it more likely that the propagule roots will drag in the mud when the tide goes in and out. The tiny roots grab the mud and plant themselves. If the propagule does not take root after about a month, it can once again float horizontally. It can float for a year or more looking for a good place to grow.

Keystone or Invasive?

The red mangrove is important to its habitat and many of the species that live there. The underwater roots of the mangroves form a nursery area, where young fish can grow and hide from predators. The trees also provide nesting places and food sources for several birds. Even their dead leaves that fall in the water play an important role. As the leaves **decompose**, they provide food for crabs, worms, shrimp, and other small animals.

Red mangroves also help to protect the coasts that they live on. Their numerous prop roots **stabilize** the soil where they grow. The coastlines can hold firm against erosion even when hurricanes bring high winds and waves ashore. The trees also take the impact of waves during storms, so that the land and buildings behind them may be protected from damage.

Although red mangroves are a keystone species in their **native** habitat, they can cause problems if they are introduced to other areas. Over one hundred years ago, the American Sugar Company brought red mangroves from Florida to Hawaii to help control erosion. Unfortunately, the trees grew quickly and crowded out the native plants. They spread to riverbanks, and their roots slowed the natural flow of rivers. Their falling leaves disrupted the balance of oxygen and nutrients in the water.

Red mangrove trees have become invasive in Hawaii and conservationists are now working to remove them. But it is important to keep these trees healthy in their natural homes. They are common in their native environments, however that does not mean that they are not threatened. Scientists estimate that the number of red mangroves declined by 17 percent from 1980 to 2007.[3] People remove the mangroves to clear the land for construction, or to use the water to raise fish. Pollutants that wash into the water can kill mangroves. While the red mangroves often help protect the coastline during hurricanes, the trees can also be destroyed by strong winds and waves.

Red mangroves are an important part of a complex ecosystem. If we can find a way to keep pollutants out of the waters and leave the trees in place, they can continue to nurture small ocean animals and protect us from damaging storms.

Living Rock Neighborhoods

Coral reefs look like huge rock formations that stick out into the ocean from the underwater shoreline. It is hard to see that they are alive and growing. But corals are actually tiny living animals with mouths and tentacles. The tentacles catch plankton and pull it into the mouth. Many corals also connect to each other. Reef-building corals build protective skeletons underneath themselves which attach to rocks or other hard surfaces. These hard shells remain when the coral builds a new skeleton under itself. A coral reef can form and grow over thousands of years. Only the corals on the top layer of the reef are still alive.

Chapter 5

OCHRE SEA STAR

If you saw a picture labeled "ochre (OH-ker) sea star," you could be a little confused. You might even say, "Wait, that's a starfish, not a sea star." And you would be both right and wrong. People have called these star-shaped creatures starfish for hundreds of years. However, they are not fish. They do not have scales, fins, or backbones like fish do. They have interesting behaviors and abilities that fish do not have. For that reason, many scientists prefer to call them sea stars.

A sea star is an **echinoderm**, so it is more closely related to a sand dollar or a sea urchin than it is to a fish. There are around two thousand known species of sea stars in all of the world's oceans. Most sea stars have five arms, but there are species with as many as forty arms.

The Original Keystone Species

Ochre sea stars live along the Pacific coast from southern Alaska to northern Mexico. The species became famous among scientists in 1969 when zoology professor Robert Paine published a paper about keystone species. In 1963, Paine had begun experimenting with ochre sea stars living along the Washington state coast. He removed the

These ochre sea stars are attached to rocks along the coast of Cannon Beach, Oregon, during low tide. During high tide, the water will cover them. Ochre sea stars are more tolerant of being exposed to air than most other sea stars. They regularly live out of water for eight hours during low tide.

sea stars from an area and waited to see what happened. Paine discovered that mussels completely took over the coastline area and crowded out other species. Ochre sea stars find mussels to be very tasty. Without sea stars to eat many of the mussels, the mussels were free to reproduce and eat everything in sight. The number of species in the area was cut in half in less than a year.[1]

Paine called the sea stars a keystone species. When he removed the sea stars from that coastline area, the whole ecosystem collapsed. The natural balance among ochre sea stars, mussels, and the other species was destroyed.

Moving, Eating, and Regrowing Body Parts

Ochre sea stars usually have five arms attached to a central disc. Their top sides are covered with short spines. They range from six to twenty inches (fifteen to fifty centimeters) across. Ochre sea stars can be yellow, orange, brown, or reddish, but the most common color for these sea stars is purple. For that reason, they are sometimes called purple sea stars. They travel slowly on strong tube feet that attach to the rocks like suction cups. They live in coastal areas, and they can survive out of water for short periods of time during low tide.

Ochre sea stars are carnivores. They grasp their prey, often mussels, and pry open the shells just a crack with their tube feet. Then the sea star turns its stomach inside out and pushes it out through its mouth. The stomach can fit through very small openings. Once inside the mussel's slightly opened shell, the stomach uses its strong digestive juices to dissolve the meat. The sea star's stomach then pulls itself out of the shell, full of liquid mussel. Although ochre sea stars love mussels, they will also eat chitons,

Water pressure powers the tiny tube feet on the underside of an ochre sea star. Water enters the sea star through small plates on its top side, and the water travels to the tube feet through canals in the sea star's arms. By turning the water pressure in a tube foot on or off, the sea star can cause the tube foot to extend and grab a rock or other surface, or release it.

tube feet

limpets, snails, clams, and barnacles when mussels are not available.

Echinoderms do not have blood. Instead, they have a water **vascular** system. Seawater flows through a network of canals in the body and arms of the sea stars. Sea stars do not have brains or eyes. They do have organs called eyespots at the tip of each arm. These eyespots can detect light, but they don't see the way human eyes do. When a sea star is deciding where to go, usually a single arm leads the way across the ocean floor.

Like other sea stars, the ochre can regrow parts of its body. If an ochre sea star loses one of its arms, it can regrow a new one. It only needs one arm remaining and the central disk to perform this magic. It can take up to a year for the process to work, but the sea star will recover completely.

The Life of a Sea Star

Ochre sea stars reproduce in late spring or early summer by a process called spawning. Females release as many as

This ochre sea star has one arm that is much shorter than the other four. It appears to be in the process of regrowing its arm after an unfortunate meeting with a predator. Sometimes regrown arms do not look exactly like the others, but they function normally.

forty million eggs into the water, and males release **sperm** into the water. If a sperm meets an egg, the egg will be **fertilized**. Fertilized eggs become tiny larvae, which feed on plankton. These larvae go through several stages before they undergo **metamorphosis** to become adults.

Adult ochre sea stars continue to grow throughout their lives when the food supply is good. Their life span depends on how much food is available, but ochre sea stars may live as long as twenty years. As adults they have few enemies, but sea otters and sea gulls do eat them.

Sick Sea Stars

Ochre sea stars are common in their range, and they are not endangered. But recently scientists have discovered that something is killing ochre sea stars along with several other sea star species.

Marine **ecologist** Steven Fradkin was startled to see some very sick sea stars at Starfish Point, northwest of Seattle, Washington, in June 2013. Many of the sea stars had sores on their bodies. The animals' internal organs were coming through their skins. Fradin later said that the worst sight was sea star arms that had ripped away from their bodies. "There were individual arms just roaming around," he said.[2]

The die-off of sea stars continued to alarm scientists, who hurried to find the cause of sea-star wasting disease. Early tests showed a link to a type of virus. It also seemed to scientists that climate change might be adding to the problem. Gases like carbon dioxide can be absorbed from the air into the ocean, changing the water's chemistry. Warming ocean temperatures might also be making the disease worse. Right now, scientists don't know for sure what is causing sea-star wasting disease, and they have no treatment for it.

There is some good news. In 2014, large batches of baby sea stars were found.[3] Although the ochre sea star is not out of the woods yet, it may be on its way.

Brightly-colored ochre sea stars are not just fun to see on rocky beaches. They are also the original keystone species. Their very important job keeps their ecosystem in balance. Humans might not have a cure for their disease yet, but we can work together to keep our oceans clean and healthy. If we do that, hopefully the ochre sea stars will be around to continue keeping their ecosystem in balance.

The Sea Cucumber

An animal called a cucumber might make you think of the fruit with the same name. Some sea cucumbers do look like the cucumbers that you could buy in the supermarket. But sea cucumbers are echinoderms like sea stars and sea urchins. They live in oceans around the world and eat all kinds of tiny debris they find on the ocean floor. Some species bury themselves in the ocean floor or hide between rocks. They push feathery tentacles out into the water, which are used to catch their dinners. If they sense a predator nearby, they pull their tentacles back into their bodies and disappear beneath the sand or rocks. Other sea cucumbers try to escape their predators by shooting sticky poisonous threads out of their rear ends. The missing threads regrow quickly.

CHAPTER NOTES

Chapter 1: Tiger Shark

1. State of Hawai'i, "Shark Incidents: Incidents List," http://dlnr.hawaii.gov/sharks/shark-incidents/incidents-list/

2. Hawai'i State Department of Health, *Injuries in Hawai'i*, 2007-2011, "Fatal Drownings and Near Drownings," September 2012, p. 188, http://health.hawaii.gov/injuryprevention/files/2013/10/Databook-FINAL-Sept-2012.pdf

3. Nova Southeastern University, Guy Harvey Research Institute, "Tracking Tiger Shark (*Galeocerdo cuvier*) Migrations in the Western North and Central Atlantic Ocean," http://www.nova.edu/ocean/ghri/tiger-sharks/

4. Kyah Draper, "*Galeocerdo cuvier*: Leopard Shark (Also: Tiger Shark)," University of Michigan Museum of Zoology, *Animal Diversity Web*, February 13, 2011, http://animaldiversity.org/accounts/Galeocerdo_cuvier/

5. C. Simpfendorfer, "*Galeocerdo cuvier*," The IUCN Red List of Threatened Species, 2009, http://www.iucnredlist.org/details/39378/0

6. Ibid.

7. Draper, "*Galeocerdo cuvier*: Leopard Shark."

8. Ibid.

9. Aaron J. Wirsing, Michael R. Heithaus, and Lawrence M. Dill, "Living on the Edge: Dugongs Prefer to Forage in Microhabitats that Allow Escape from Rather than Avoidance of Predators," *Animal Behaviour*, 2007, pp. 93-101, http://citeseerx.ist.psu.edu/viewdoc/download?doi=10.1.1.379.4208&rep=rep1&type=pdf

10. Darren Naish, "Tales From the *Cryptozoologicon*: Megalodon!," *Scientific American*, August 5, 2013, http://blogs.scientificamerican.com/tetrapod-zoology/2013/08/05/cryptozoologicon-megalodon-teaser/

Chapter 2: Sea Otter

1. Clarence R. Robbins, *Chemical and Physical Behavior of Human Hair*, Fifth Edition (New York: Springer, 2012), p. 26.

2. Rachel A. Kuhn, Hermann Ansorge, Szymon Godynicki, and Wilfried Meyer, "Hair Density in the Eurasian Otter *Lutra lutra* and the Sea Otter *Enhydra lutris*," *Acta Theriologica*, September 2010, pp. 211-222.

3. A. Doroff and A. Burdin, "*Enhydra lutris*," The IUCN Red List of Threatened Species, 2013, http://www.iucnredlist.org/details/7750/0

4. Jess Righthand, "Picky Eaters," *Smithsonian*, September 2011, pp. 1-2, from Academic Search Elite.

5. MarineBio Conservation Society, "Sea Otters, *Enhydra lutris*," January 14, 2013, http://marinebio.org/species.asp?id=157

6. John Nielsen, "Killer Whales Thinning Otter Populations," *All Things Considered*, NPR, May 24, 2005, http://www.npr.org/templates/story/story.php?storyId=4665067

7. Righthand, "Picky Eaters."

8. Doroff and Burdin, "*Enhydra lutris*."

9. Point Defiance Zoo and Aquarium, "Sea Otter Homer, Believed to Be the Last Remaining Exxon Valdez Oil Spill Survivor of Her Species, Humanely Euthanized at Point Defiance Zoo & Aquarium," June 24, 2013, http://www.pdza.org/file_viewer.php?id=5903

Chapter 3: Antarctic Krill

1. Antarctic and Southern Ocean Coalition, "Krill Conservation," http://www.asoc.org/advocacy/krill-conservation

2. Rachel Gierak, "*Euphausia superba*: Antarctic Krill," *Animal Diversity Web*, University of Michigan Museum of Zoology, October 12, 2013, http://animaldiversity.org/accounts/Euphausia_superba/

3. Ibid.

4. Kenneth Brower, "Life in Antarctica Relies on Shrinking Supply of Krill," *National Geographic*, August 17, 2013, http://news.nationalgeographic.com/news/2013/08/130817-antarctica-krill-whales-ecology-climate-science/

5. Wendy Rockliffe and Steve Nicol, "Krill: Magicians of the Southern Ocean," Australian Antarctic Division, August 12, 2010, http://www.antarctica.gov.au/about-antarctica/wildlife/animals/krill/krill-magicians-of-the-southern-ocean

6. Gierak, "*Euphausia superba*: Antarctic Krill."

7. Ibid.

8. Brower, "Life in Antarctica Relies on Shrinking Supply of Krill."

Chapter 4: Red Mangrove

1. IUCN, "Mangrove Forests in Worldwide Decline," April 9, 2010, http://www.iucn.org/?5025/Mangrove-forests-in-worldwide-decline

2. Global Invasive Species Database, "*Rhizophora mangle* (Aquatic Plant, Tree, Shrub)," July 31, 2007, http://www.issg.org/database/species/ecology.asp?si=1164&fr=1

3. A. Ellison, E. Farnsworth, and G. Moore, "*Rhizophora mangle*," The IUCN Red List of Threatened Species, 2010, http://www.iucnredlist.org/details/178851/0

Chapter 5: Ochre Sea Star

1. Ed Yong, "Scientific Families: Dynasty," *Nature*, January 16, 2013, http://www.nature.com/news/scientific-families-dynasty-1.12205

2. Elizabeth Lopatto, "In Search of the Starfish Killer: The Quest to Save the Original Keystone Species," *Verge*, November 18, 2014, http://www.theverge.com/2014/11/18/7222479/starfish-wasting-quest-save-keystone-species

3. Ibid.

WORKS CONSULTED

Allegra, Joe, Rhiannon Rath, and Aren Gunderson. "*Enhydra lutris*: Sea Otter." University of Michigan Museum, *Animal Diversity Web*, October 3, 2012. http://animaldiversity.org/accounts/enhydra_lutris/

Antarctic and Southern Ocean Coalition. "Krill Conservation." http://www.asoc.org/advocacy/krill-conservation

Bird, Jonathan. "Echinoderms, the Spiny Animals!" Oceanic Research Group, June 5, 2007. http://www.oceanicresearch.org/education/wonders/echinoderm.html

Brower, Kenneth. "Life in Antarctica Relies on Shrinking Supply of Krill." *National Geographic*, August 17, 2013. http://news.nationalgeographic.com/news/2013/08/130817-antarctica-krill-whales-ecology-climate-science/

Doroff, A. and A. Burdin. "*Enhydra lutris*." The IUCN Red List of Threatened Species, 2013. http://www.iucnredlist.org/details/7750/0

Draper, Kyah. "*Galeocerdo cuvier*: Leopard Shark (Also: Tiger Shark)." University of Michigan Museum of Zoology, *Animal Diversity Web*, February 13, 2011. http://animaldiversity.org/accounts/Galeocerdo_cuvier/

Ellison, A., E. Farnsworth, and G. Moore. "*Rhizophora mangle*." The IUCN Red List of Threatened Species, 2010. http://www.iucnredlist.org/details/178851/0

Food and Agriculture Organization of the United Nations. "*Euphausia superba*." http://www.fao.org/fishery/species/3393/en

Gierak, Rachel. "*Euphausia superba*: Antarctic Krill." *Animal Diversity Web*, University of Michigan Museum of Zoology, October 12, 2013. http://animaldiversity.org/accounts/Euphausia_superba/

Global Invasive Species Database. "*Rhizophora mangle* (Aquatic Plant, Tree, Shrub)." July 31, 2007. http://www.issg.org/database/species/ecology.asp?si=1164&fr=1

Goldberg, W. "Antarctic Krill: A Keystone Species." Florida International University, 2005. http://www2.fiu.edu/~goldberg/marinebio/Euphausiasuperba.htm

Griffin, E., K. L. Miller, B. Freitas, and M. Hirshfield. "Predators as Prey: Why Healthy Oceans Need Sharks." Oceana, July 2008. http://oceana.org/sites/default/files/reports/Predators_as_Prey_FINAL_FINAL1.pdf

Hawai'i State Department of Health. *Injuries in Hawai'i*, 2007-2011. "Fatal Drownings and Near Drownings." September 2012. http://health.hawaii.gov/injuryprevention/files/2013/09/drowning_Datachapter2007-11a-1MB.pdf

International Science and Health Foundation. "Krill Facts Center." http://www.krillfacts.org/1-krill-facts-center.html

IUCN. "Mangrove Forests in Worldwide Decline." April 9, 2010. http://www.iucn.org/?5025/Mangrove-forests-in-worldwide-decline

Kew Royal Botanic Gardens. "*Rhizophora mangle* (Red Mangrove)." http://www.kew.org/science-conservation/plants-fungi/rhizophora-mangle-red-mangrove

Knickle, Craig. "Tiger Shark." Florida Museum of Natural History. https://www.flmnh.ufl.edu/fish/Gallery/Descript/tigershark/tigershark.htm

Kuhn, Rachel A., Hermann Ansorge, Szymon Godynicki, and Wilfried Meyer. "Hair Density in the Eurasian Otter *Lutra lutra* and the Sea Otter *Enhydra lutris*." *Acta Theriologica*, September 2010, pp. 211-222.

Lopatto, Elizabeth. "In Search of the Starfish Killer: The Quest to Save the Original Keystone Species." *Verge*, November 18, 2014. http://www.theverge.com/2014/11/18/7222479/starfish-wasting-quest-save-keystone-species

MarineBio Conservation Society. "Sea Otters, *Enhydra lutris*." January 14, 2013. http://marinebio.org/species.asp?id=157

------. "Tiger Sharks, *Galeocerdo cuvier*." January 14, 2013. http://marinebio.org/species.asp?id=37

Mulcrone, Renee Sherman. "Echinodermata: Sea Stars, Sea Urchins, Sea Cucumbers, and Relatives." University of Michigan Museum of Zoology, *Animal Diversity Web*, January 29, 2005. http://animaldiversity.org/accounts/Echinodermata/

Naish, Darren. "Tales From the *Cryptozoologicon*: Megalodon!" *Scientific American*, August 5, 2013. http://blogs.scientificamerican.com/tetrapod-zoology/2013/08/05/cryptozoologicon-megalodon-teaser/

National Geographic. "Sea Cucumber." http://animals.nationalgeographic.com/animals/invertebrates/sea-cucumber/

------. "Starfish (Sea Star)." http://animals.nationalgeographic.com/animals/invertebrates/starfish/

National Oceanic and Atmospheric Administration. "Ecosystems: Kelp Forests." June 21, 2013. http://sanctuaries.noaa.gov/about/ecosystems/kelpdesc.html

------. "*Pisaster ochraceus*: Ochre Sea Star." http://www.sanctuarysimon.org/species/pisaster/ochraceus/ochre-sea-star

------. "What Are Coral Reefs." Coral Reef Information System, December 16, 2014. http://www.coris.noaa.gov/about/what_are/

WORKS CONSULTED

Newton, Steven. "Megalodon Bites Back—How the Discovery Channel Sank Its Credibility." *Huffington Post*, August 8, 2013. http://www.huffingtonpost.com/steven-newton/megalodon-shark-week_b_3721329.html

Nicol, Stephen. "Time to Krill?" Australian Antarctic Division. http://www.eco-action.org/dt/timeto.html

Nielsen, John. "Killer Whales Thinning Otter Populations." *All Things Considered*, NPR, May 24, 2005. http://www.npr.org/templates/story/story.php?storyId=4665067

Nova Southeastern University, Guy Harvey Research Institute. "Tracking Tiger Shark (*Galeocerdo cuvier*) Migrations in the Western North and Central Atlantic Ocean." http://www.nova.cdu/ocean/ghri/tiger-sharks/

Ombrello, Dr. T. "Red Mangrove." Union County College, Department of Biology. http://faculty.ucc.edu/biology-ombrello/POW/red_mangrove.htm

Otter Project. "Biology of the Southern Sea Otter." http://www.otterproject.org/about-sea-otters/biology-of-the-southern-sea-otter/

Point Defiance Zoo and Aquarium. "Sea Otter Homer, Believed to Be the Last Remaining Exxon Valdez Oil Spill Survivor of Her Species, Humanely Euthanized at Point Defiance Zoo & Aquarium." June 24, 2013. http://www.pdza.org/file_viewer.php?id=5903

Ramirez, Yesenia. "*Pisaster ochraceus*." University of Michigan Museum of Zoology, *Animal Diversity Web*, February 26, 2002. http://animaldiversity.org/accounts/Pisaster_ochraceus/

Righthand, Jess. "Picky Eaters." *Smithsonian*, September 2011, pp. 1–4. From Academic Search Elite.

Robbins, Clarence R. *Chemical and Physical Behavior of Human Hair*, Fifth Edition. New York: Springer, 2012.

Rockliffe, Wendy, and Steve Nicol. "Krill: Magicians of the Southern Ocean." Australian Antarctic Division, August 12, 2010. http://www.antarctica.gov.au/about-antarctica/wildlife/animals/krill/krill-magicians-of-the-southern-ocean

Simpfendorfer, C. "*Galeocerdo cuvier*." The IUCN Red List of Threatened Species, 2009. http://www.iucnredlist.org/details/39378/0

Slater Museum of Natural History, University of Puget Sound. "Ochre Sea Star (*Pisaster ochraceus*)." http://www.pugetsound.edu/academics/academic-resources/slater-museum/exhibits/marine-panel/ochre-sea-star/

State of Hawai'i. "Shark Incidents: Incidents List." http://dlnr.hawaii.gov/sharks/shark-incidents/incidents-list/

US Fish and Wildlife Service. "Mangroves: Multi-Species Recovery Plan for South Florida." http://www.fws.gov/verobeach/msrppdfs/mangroves.pdf

Ward, Paul. "Blue Whale—*Balaenoptera musculus*." Cool Antarctica, 2001. http://www.coolantarctica.com/Antarctica%20fact%20file/wildlife/whales/blue_whale.htm

Wirsing, Aaron J., Michael R. Heithaus, and Lawrence M. Dill. "Living on the Edge: Dugongs Prefer to Forage in Microhabitats that Allow Escape from Rather than Avoidance of Predators." *Animal Behaviour*, 2007, pp. 93–101. http://citeseerx.ist.psu.edu/viewdoc/download?doi=10.1.1.379.4208&rep=rep1&type=pdf

Yong, Ed. "Scientific Families: Dynasty." *Nature*, January 16, 2013. http://www.nature.com/news/scientific-families-dynasty-1.12205

FURTHER READING

Gilpin, Daniel. *Starfish, Urchins, and Other Echinoderms*. Mankato, MN: Compass Point Books, 2006.

Nuzzolo, Deborah. *Tiger Shark*. Mankato, MN: Capstone Press, 2011.

Parker, Steve. *Ocean and Sea*. New York: Scholastic, 2012.

Slade, Suzanne. *What If There Were No Sea Otters? A Book About the Ocean Ecosystem*. Mankato, MN: Picture Window Books, 2011.

Taylor, Barbara. *Arctic and Antarctic*. New York: DK Publishing, 2012.

ON THE INTERNET

British Antarctic Survey: Halley Research Station (with information about living in an Antarctic research center and several videos and webcams) http://www.antarctica.ac.uk/living_and_working/research_stations/halley/index.php

Krill Facts: Kid's Center http://www.krillfacts.org/3-kid-s-center.html

Monterey Bay Aquarium: Sea Otter Cam http://www.montereybayaquarium.org/animals-and-experiences/live-web-cams/sea-otter-cam

Nova Southeastern University: Online Shark Tracking http://www.nova.edu/ocean/ghri/tracking/

Time For Kids: Antarctica http://www.timeforkids.com/minisite/Antarctica

GLOSSARY

aerial (AIR-ee-uhl)—living in the air

apex predator (EY-peks PRED-uh-ter)—a predator at the top of its food chain, having no predators

benthic (BEN-thik)—relating to the region at the bottom of a lake, sea, or ocean

blunt—having a rounded, dull edge

carnivorous (kahr-NIV-er-uhs)—eating meat

conservationist (kon-ser-VEY-shuh-nist)—a person who works to protect and restore natural resources like animals, plants, streams, and oceans

crustacean (kruh-STEY-shuhn)—a member of a species that lives in water and has a hard shell, like a lobster, shrimp, crab, or crayfish

decompose (dee-kuhm-POHZ)—to rot or to break down

delicacy (DEL-i-kuh-see)—a food that is very rare or expensive

dramatize (DRAH-muh-tahyz)—to make ready for a performance or show, often by adding untrue information to create a more interesting story

dugong (DOO-gong)—an ocean-dwelling mammal with a barrel-shaped body, flipperlike front legs, and no back legs

echinoderm (EK-uh-nuh-durm)—a marine animal with parts that radiate out from the center; includes sea stars, sea urchins, and sea cucumbers

ecologist (ih-KOL-uh-jist)—a scientist who studies the relationships between living organisms and their environment

ecosystem (EE-koh-sis-tuhm)—a system of interaction of the plants and animals in a community

epoch (EP-uhk)—a period of time in the geologic history of Earth

fertilize (FUR-tuhl-ahyz)—to bring together the male sperm and the female egg to develop into offspring

gestation (je-STEY-shuhn)—the length of time of pregnancy

habitat (HAB-i-tat)—the place where a plant or animal naturally lives and grows

hemisphere (HEM-i-sfeer)—half of the earth, divided along the equator

invertebrate (in-VUR-tuh-brit)—an animal without a backbone

larvae (LAHR-vuh)—the young of an invertebrate animal

litter (LIT-er)—a group of babies that an animal has at the same birth

metamorphosis (met-uh-MAWR-fuh-sis)—a change in the form of an organism

native (NEY-tiv)—currently living in the place where it originally lived (as in a species of plant or animal)

parasite (PAR-uh-sahyt)—a living organism that lives on or in a host organism and receives food from its host

pelt—the raw hide or skin of an animal

protein (PROH-teen)—a molecule that is used by a plant or animal to grow and maintain its body

range—the area that the population of a species lives in

reef—a ridge of rock or sand at or near the surface of a body of water

serrated (suh-REY-tid)—having a notched edge like a saw

sperm (spurm)—a male reproductive cell

stabilize (STEY-buh-lahyz)—to make something constant or able to resist change

tolerate (TOL-uh-reyt)—to experience a hardship

vascular (VAS-kyuh-ler)—related to the tubes or ducts that transport fluids such as blood, lymph, or sap

INDEX

About the Author

Bonnie Hinman has loved studying nature since she was a child growing up on her family's farm. Today she is a certified Missouri Master Naturalist and works in her community educating children and adults about the natural world around them. She also volunteers her time to restore and maintain the local ecosystem. Hinman has had more than thirty books published including Mitchell Lane's *Threat to the Leatherback Turtle*. She lives with her husband Bill in Joplin, Missouri, near her children and five grandchildren.

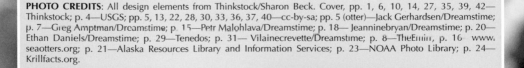